Buildings in Asia

Lisa James

Contents

Buildings

In Asia there are many kinds of buildings.

They are used for all sorts of things.

Let's take a look at some of the most interesting buildings in Asia.

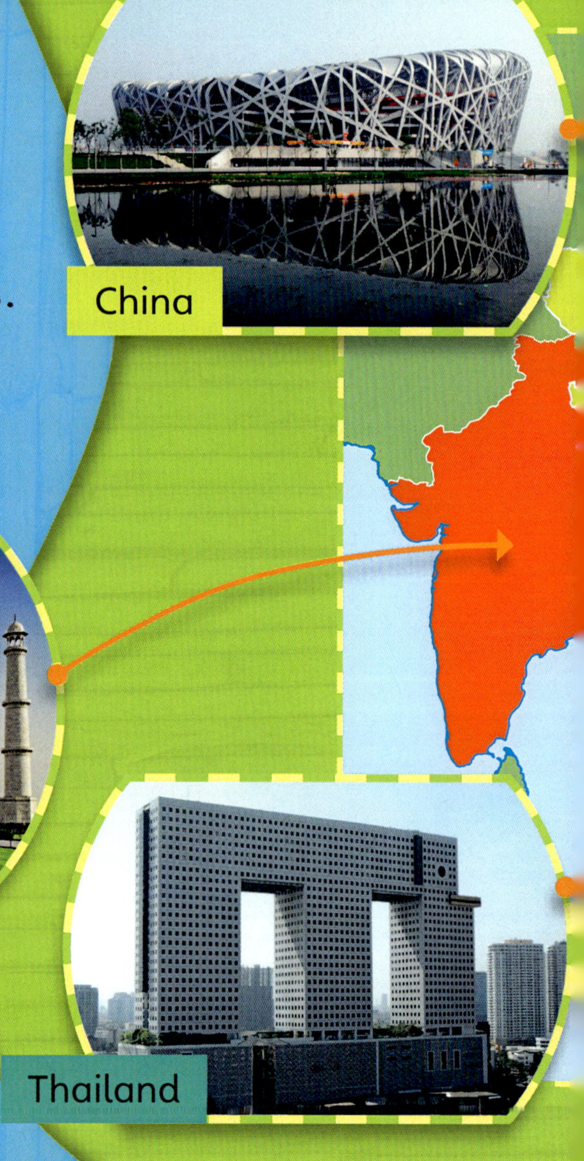

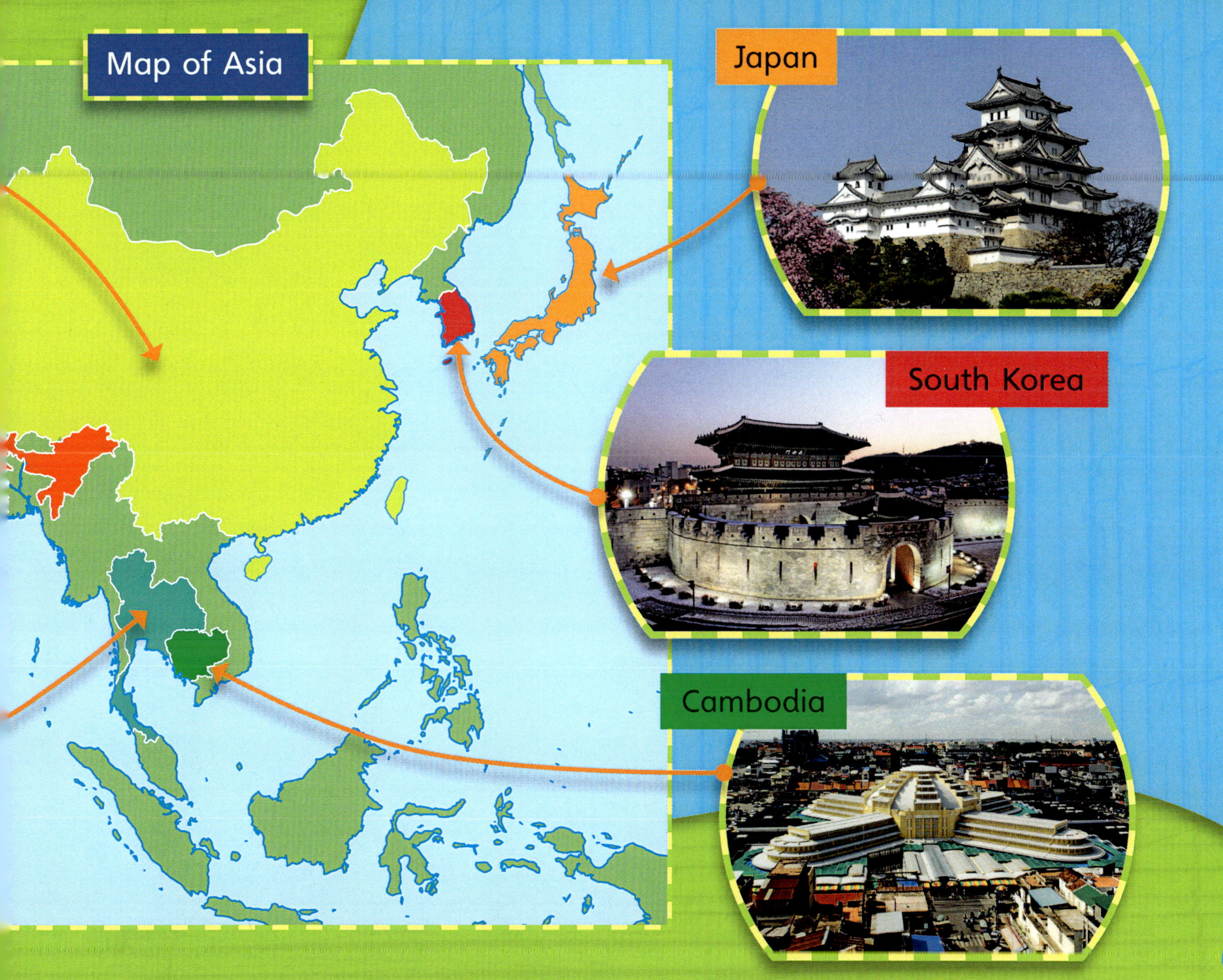
Map of Asia
Japan
South Korea
Cambodia

China

This building is a **palace**.
It was built hundreds of years ago.
It was a home for Chinese **emperors**.

This building is a **stadium**.
It is sometimes called the "Bird's Nest".
Do you think it looks like a bird's nest?

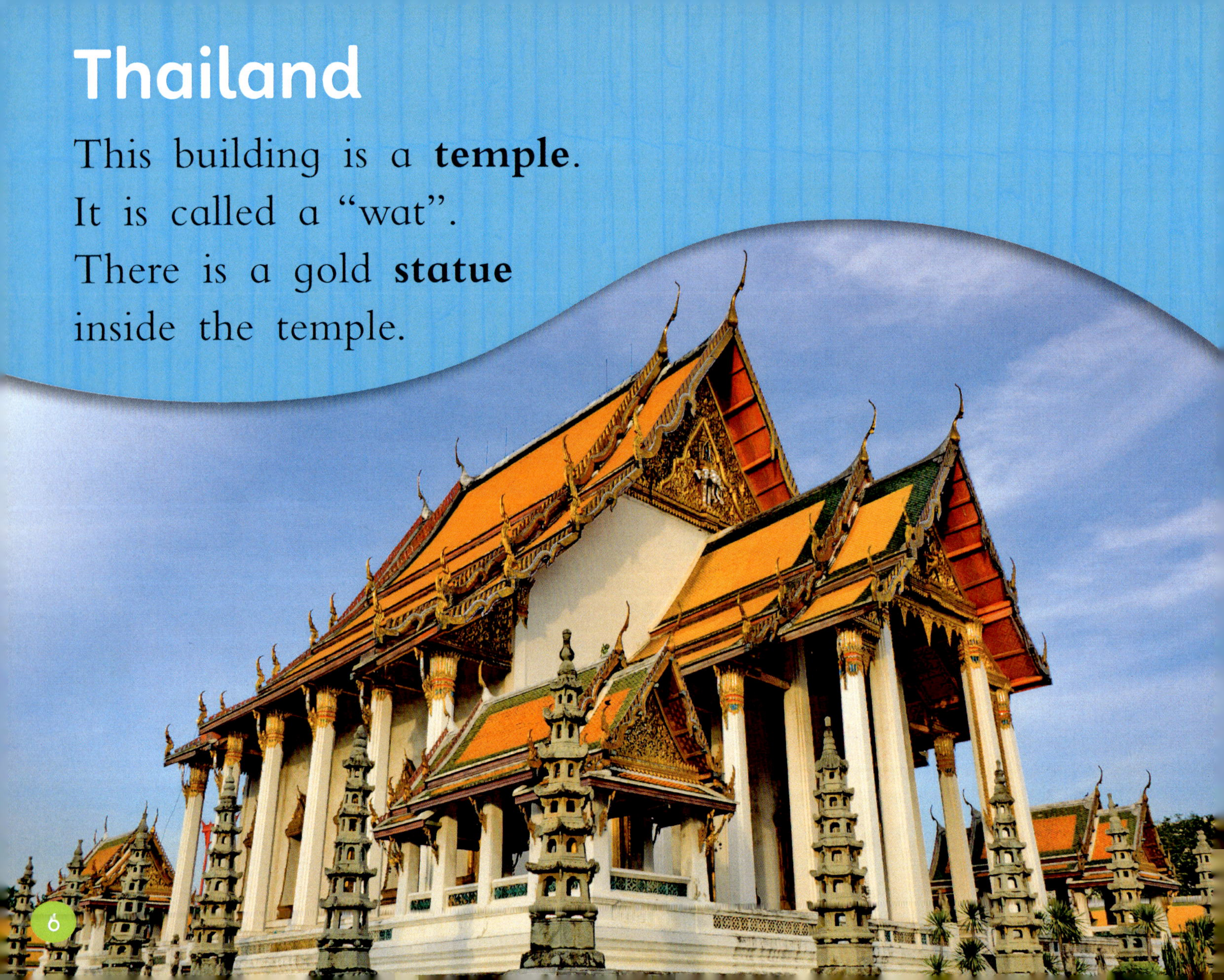

Thailand

This building is a **temple**. It is called a "wat". There is a gold **statue** inside the temple.

This building is a **skyscraper**.
It is called the Elephant Building.
Can you see why?

Japan

This building is a **castle**.
It was built on top of a hill.
Some people think it looks like a white bird.
Do you?

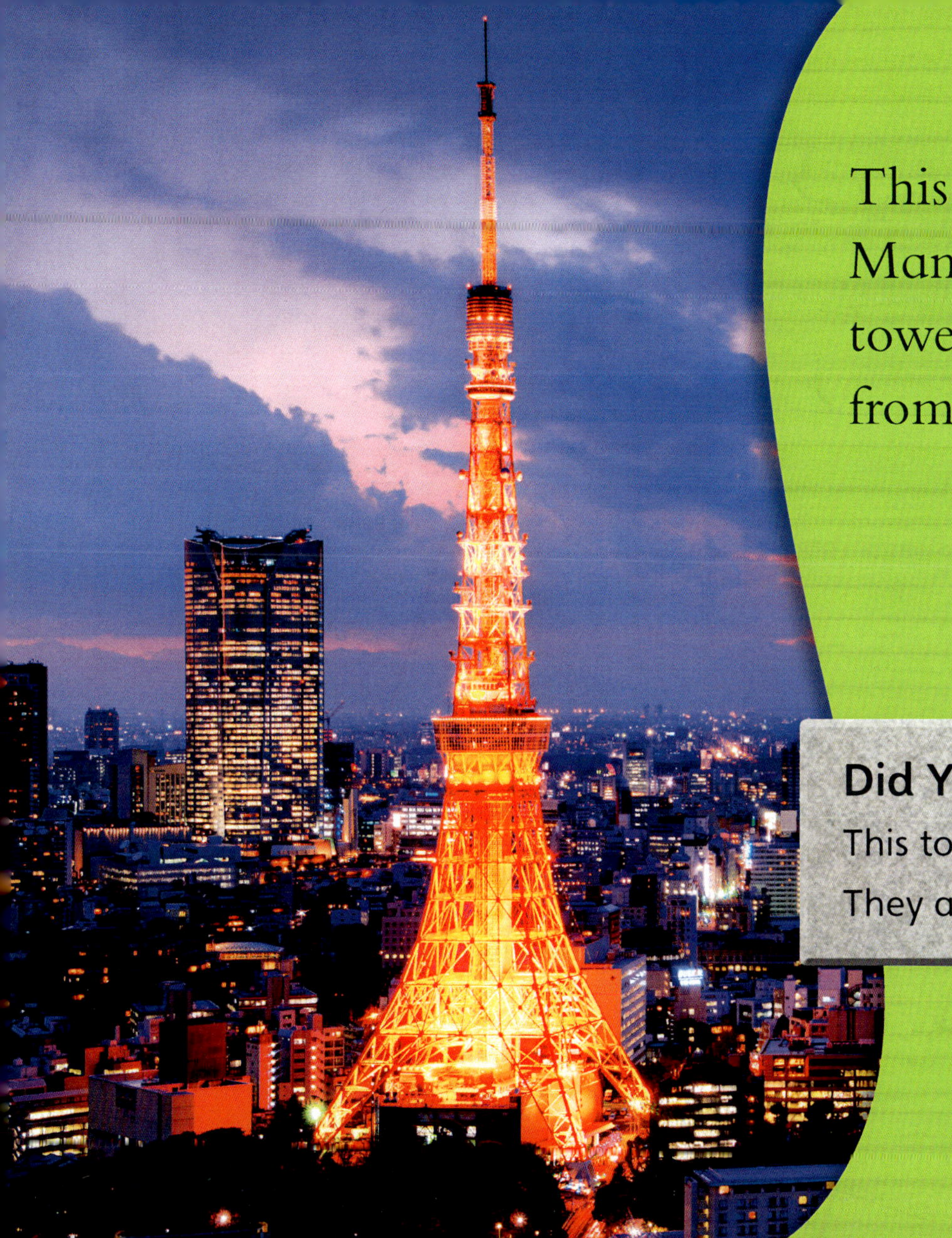

This building is a **tower**. Many people climb the tower to see the city from above.

Did You Know?

This tower has 176 lights. They are turned on at night.

Cambodia

This building is a temple.
It was not used for a long time.
Now, people come from all over the world to see it.

This building is a **market**.
It has four big arms.
People buy all sorts of things there.

South Korea

This building is a **fort**.
The walls of the fort are high and strong.
This keeps the people inside safe.

This building is a skyscraper.
It is 249 metres tall.
The windows are made of glass that looks like gold.

Did You Know?

This building has 63 floors.
Three of the floors are under the ground.

India

This building is a **monument**.
It was built by an emperor.
It took over 20 years to build.

This building is a **hotel**.
It has a palace and a tower.
There are 565 rooms where people can stay.

Glossary

castle	a large, strong building
emperors	rulers or leaders
fort	a building made to keep people safe, often with a high wall around it
hotel	a place where people stay when they are away from home
market	a place where food and useful items are sold
monument	a building or structure made to remember an important person or event
palace	the home of a royal family or leader of a country
skyscraper	a very tall building with many levels
stadium	a place to watch sports or enjoy concerts
statue	a figure made from materials like stone or wood
temple	a building for prayer
tower	a tall, narrow building